THE FRANCHISE REVOLUTION

The 6 Principles every Franchisor must follow to successfully franchise in the 21st Century

Susan-Ann Hills

To Jo,

with very Best

wishes

Suy

x

1

"Sue has created a fresh new approach to franchising, putting people before procedures and encouraging partnerships that flourish. A must read for both new and established franchisors"

Sean Cragg
UK Operations Director at Nua Healthcare Services

Copyright

"The Franchise Revolution: The 6 Principles every franchisor must follow to successfully franchise in the 21st Century "

Written by: Susan-Ann Hills

Copyright © 2013 by Susan-Ann Hills

Published by **Bright Future Publishing Ltd**

This publication is designed to provide accurate and authoritative information in regard to the subject matter covered. It is sold on the understanding that the publisher is not engaged in rendering legal, accounting, or other professional services. If legal advice or other expert assistance is required, the services of a competent professional person should be sought.

Franchise Revolution
www.franchiserevolution.co.uk

FREE TRANSFORMATIVE FRANCHISING™ RESOURCE STARTER PACK

**INCLUDES - 7 RESOURCES
PLUS 2 BONUS GUIDES**

**DOWNLOAD YOUR RESOURCE PACK NOW AT
http://franchiserevolution.co.uk/resources**

TABLE OF CONTENTS

PART ONE

THE NEW FRANCHISING STRATEGY THAT WILL TAKE YOUR BUSINESS TO THE NEXT LEVEL OF GROWTH AND BEYOND

INTRODUCTION

THE FRANCHISE REVOLUTION

DEFINITION OF REVOLUTION:-

"A dramatic and wide-reaching change in the way something works or is organised or in people's ideas about it"

(Oxford Online Dictionary)

Franchising is a brilliant business model. I have been involved in franchising for many years and have experienced it from different perspectives. I have been both franchisor and franchisee and I have had the privilege of meeting many franchisors and franchisees on my journey.   As a result of these varied encounters, I have learned a great deal about what is good, and not so good about franchising from both the franchisor and franchisee perspectives. Whilst I firmly believe there is a lot of good practice, I also know that there is room for improvement and a huge opportunity to bring franchising into line with 21st century best business practices. I am convinced that this will result in a positive impact for both franchisor and franchisee.

Why Franchise?

The 2012 NatWest BFA Survey 2012 states that despite continuing pressures on the economy as a whole, franchising in the UK continues to expand. There will always be entrepreneurs who love creating brands and developing businesses into large profitable organisations, and there will always be aspiring business owners who want to start their own businesses but maybe haven't the desire or confidence to go it alone. They may like the idea of having regular support from the franchisor, as well as a network of other franchisees to liaise with.

There are also "entrepreneur franchisees" who enjoy the challenge of building large businesses and profits by purchasing multiple territories but are happy to do this under someone else's brand. As one franchisee said "why spend hours upon hours and heaps of money creating and building a brand when you can buy into someone else's ready-made brand and bypass all of that hard work!" When you look at it like that, he certainly has a point!

In the current economic climate, people no longer expect jobs for life, and redundancy is often the norm rather than the exception. It is also now widely predicted that people will have multiple careers during their working lifetime. Becoming a franchisee offers aspiring business owners the opportunity to run their own business and take back control of their lives and finances as well as being part of a wider network of fellow franchisees. This provides the benefit of "being in business for yourself but not by yourself". I believe that buying a franchise will become an increasingly popular future choice for people who want to start their own business. This is good news for franchisors or businesses that are considering franchising as a growth strategy as they are able to leverage franchising as a lower risk but powerful growth strategy and this is particularly attractive in today's uncertain economic times.

Why Franchising needs to Change

I have also learned from my own experience that franchising in its current form is not working as effectively as it could be, and has not significantly evolved since its inception. Despite its many advantages, franchising is often perceived as complicated, time consuming and very expensive as well as being viewed as favouring the franchisor. The latter may appeal to the franchisor, but it is important to redress any imbalances as this will attract far more franchisees into the franchise sector which is what every franchisor needs and wants in order to grow.

Today the buzzwords in business are **Digital, Engagement and Connection**. People want to feel connected which is evidenced by the phenomenal rise of social media. Franchise partnerships can be imbued with core values such as mutual trust and respect, transparency, collaboration and empowerment, all of which will result in enhanced franchisee engagement. Time and time again, research shows huge benefits for companies that have engaged employees and so it is only common sense that franchisors adopt similar strategies to enhance franchisee engagement. So, how can franchisors capitalise on this knowledge?

Transformative Franchising™

DEFINITION OF TRANSFORMATIVE:-
"Of or relating to the process of changing a person or thing into something better or more attractive"
(Collins English Online Dictionary)

Transformative Franchising™ is the key ingredient to your success in franchising and is the new paradigm for franchising now and into the future. Transformative Franchising™ recognises the importance of putting people before systems and the huge impact this can have on the success of a franchised business. Its principles are grounded in empirical studies and based on three key areas: transformational leadership; employee engagement; and best current business practices.

"Transformational Leadership is a partnership to reach a higher level of motivation, trust, engagement and empowerment."

(E J Shelton 2012)

As you read through this book, you will begin to understand just how powerful Transformative Franchising™ is and how, by adopting its principles, you can build a highly successful and sustainable franchise business whatever stage you are at. Time and time again, studies have shown that when companies adopt a transformational leadership approach, a win/win scenario unfolds for everyone involved in the company from employees to shareholders. By transferring these principles to franchising you will begin to understand the enormous power and potential of Transformative Franchising™.

Traditionally, franchising has primarily focused on systems and procedures. Yet franchising is ultimately about people. Franchisors and franchisees are at the heart of any franchise network and their actions and behaviours influence how successful the franchise is. The importance of this is all too often forgotten and in conventional franchising, systems, procedures and processes take centre stage. Transformative Franchising™ seeks to redress this by offering powerful principles to drive your franchise forward. Franchisors that continue to use "old school" strategies will be bypassed in favour of those bold franchisors that are prepared to move forward and embrace best practices from the most successful companies in the world. Franchise owners that adopt the Transformative Franchising™ model will find their businesses growing exponentially, with increased profits; sustainability and a sizeable net asset for years to come. Of equal importance, they will have created a network of harmonious and engaged franchise partners that will experience respect, recognition and fulfilment which will in turn lead to higher customer satisfaction and therefore ultimately, higher profits for everyone. Their franchise partners will also be a far more powerful recruitment marketing and advertising vehicle, therefore saving further costs as well as growing the business.

How this Book will Help You

The purpose of this book is to share with you the phenomenal power of Transformative Franchising™. We will look at why franchising needs to change; what Transformative Franchising™ is and why it is essential; comparisons between conventional franchising and Transformative Franchising™; how it works in practice and how to put it all together.

By the end of this book you will have learned:

- ✓ Why Transformative Franchising™ is the future
- ✓ How to implement Transformative Franchising™ as a very powerful growth strategy for your business
- ✓ How to develop a highly profitable and sustainable business
- ✓ How to develop a network of fully engaged franchise partners
- ✓ How to grow your network exponentially
- ✓ How to avoid the mistakes made by conventional franchising

Finally, a word of warning. This book is not like any other franchise book. It is not just a "how to franchise your business" book. It is a completely new approach to franchising. If you read this book and adopt its principles, your business will be a vanguard for all other franchises to aspire to. Now let's get started......

CHAPTER ONE

This chapter will help you to differentiate between what is and what is not a franchise and help you to recognise the different types and sectors within franchising. This will support you in deciding which type of franchise you may create.

WHAT IS FRANCHISING?

Most people have a good understanding of what a franchise is and usually think of McDonald's as the archetypal example. However, it is beneficial to briefly outline what constitutes a franchise as some businesses parade under the umbrella of being a franchise, when in fact they are not. The International Franchise Association defines franchising as:

"An agreement or license between two legally independent parties which gives a person or group of people (franchisees) the right to market a product or service using the trademark or trade name of another business (franchisor). The franchisee has the right to market a product or service using the operating methods of the franchisor. The franchisee has an obligation to pay the franchisor fees for these rights whilst the franchisor has the obligation to provide rights and support to franchisees."

Put simply, a franchise is a business that wants to expand by licensing its proven systems, methods, services or products (the franchisor) to other potential business partners (franchisees) who wish to operate a business under the same brand, usually within an allocated territory. A contract binds both parties known as the franchise agreement. The franchisee will pay an initial franchise fee followed by a regular royalty, service fee or management fee. In return, the franchisor will train and support the franchisee for the duration of the franchise agreement which is typically between five and ten years with a clause to renew. Both parties will have certain obligations to perform under the franchise agreement.

What a franchise is not

A franchise is not pyramid selling or a business advertised as a "business opportunity" nor is it a business that purely offers a license. A licensed business usually offers products or services that are licensed by the licensor to a licensee, but traded under the licensee's own company name. Generally there is little on-going support and the licensees are very much on their own.

Examples of other businesses that do not qualify as a franchise are:

1   Network marketing
2   Party planning
3   Distributorships
4   Products or services which grant a license to run a business under a brand name but without the legalities of a franchise agreement

Types of franchise

Virtually any type of product or service can potentially be franchised if
a) the pilot operation has been successful and there is enough profit margin for a franchisee to make profit after a management fee has been paid and
b) that a business format can be prescribed and replicated relatively easily by others. Franchises generally fall into five types.

1 *Management/Investment franchises* – These usually attract "white collar" ex-employees who may have been managers or working at a senior level. Examples of management franchises are estate agencies, care services, cleaning services, professional services.

2 *Retail and fast food franchises* – the owner may work within the business initially but will employ other staff as well. Franchisees may also buy several outlets employing managers to run each outlet. These can also fall within the Management/Investment category.

3 **Professional franchises** – Typically these are franchises that sell professional services e.g. accountancy, legal, professional business services. They can be solely operated or by employing others.

4 **Van or "on the job" franchises** – usually undertaken by one person and often run from home. These include services like oven cleaning, home improvement, car repair or gardening.

5 **Master franchise or area master franchise** – covering a whole country or a wide geographical area with several separate franchise territories within it. Franchisees will usually be expected to run their own pilot operation within a defined territory in the country or areas purchased, and then sell the remaining territories in their area to other franchisees. They then receive a franchise service fee or royalty from each of their franchisees and in return pay the franchisor a service fee or royalty usually based on a percentage of the turnover from the entire network including their own.

Brief History of Franchising

The term "franchise" originated in the middle ages where it was used to describe the rights of a person to govern a piece of land which was owned by the state. In the early 1800's it was used to define voting rights and later in the 1800s's franchising was used to allow local pub owners the right to be licensed to sell a particular brewery's beer. This system is still prevalent today and is known as the "tied system".

Franchising, as we understand it today, originated in the United States with the Singer Sewing company in the mid-1800s. Singer could not cope with the large geographical demand for sales and servicing of their machines and therefore franchised the right for people to own and run independent outlets, servicing the local community of Singer Sewing machine owners, under Singer's control and direction. General Motors took a similar path as they established a network of dealerships to support the owners of their vehicles.

This concept began to develop further, when businesses realised the potential franchising could offer. Some of the early adopters included The Lyons Corner House (which included a Wimpy Bar in the premises). Wimpy Bars were so successful that they began to operate as separate outlets. However, the example most people think of when asked about franchising is of course McDonald's.

Franchising developed into the format we know today in the 1950's and has continued to grow and develop since then. Both the International Franchise Association and The British Franchise Association have played a pivotal role in ensuring that illegal and corrupt practices have been eradicated, and have set good practice guidelines for businesses to follow. (C. Sawyer, 2011).

CHAPTER TWO

What is Transformative Franchising™?

Background

Most people understand that franchising, at its grass roots level, is a business growth model that can be fairly easily taught and replicated by others following specific steps. This concept sounds relatively simple. When these steps are followed, preferably under advice of a franchise consultancy the process should be plain sailing. However, this is often not the case. During research for my previous book "**37 Insider Secrets to Buying the Right Franchise" (get the book for free at http://franchiserevolution.co.uk/resources)** I was astounded by the dissatisfaction expressed from the number of franchisees that I interviewed for case studies for the book across a wide variety of different sectors.

I also interviewed a cross section of both business and personal colleagues to gain their perspective on franchising. Again, the feedback was rather negative, particularly around their view of franchisees who they believed were exploited by the franchisor. One person even asked me if I could change the name from franchising to something more acceptable as merely the name made her shudder and another described it as the "Black Art"! These assumptions certainly do not bode well for the future of franchising.

Do only Franchisors Benefit?

It became clear that whilst most people viewed franchising as a good business model, they also felt that there was a lot wrong with it. The most common belief was that it was only the franchisor that benefited from the model and that there were often imbalances of power. It also did not appear to be a win/win partnership. This viewpoint was substantiated by many franchisees who felt that the whole model was too biased towards the franchisor. Whilst they acknowledged that the franchisor had developed the business format, they felt that their own skillset, expertise, past experiences and financial investment was often negated making them feel devalued. This resulted in de-motivation leading to lower profits which sometimes resulted in a lack of respect and trust towards the franchisor.

Franchising from the Inside-Out

This knowledge led me to review my own earlier research that I had acquired over many years of investigating franchises both in the United Kingdom and internationally. I also re-examined my previous experience of being a franchisor, in order to gain further insight into why franchising was not as successful as the business model suggests it should be. Most importantly were my experiences of being a franchisee from the "inside-out". During this time, I played a pivotal role in ensuring that channels of communication were kept open between the franchisor and franchisees. This gave me an invaluable insight into the relationship dynamics between the franchisor and franchisee, which is so fundamental to the successful on-going development of any franchise network. This experience was integral to the creation of Transformative Franchising™.

Transformative Franchising™ was created from both my own and other's experiences of franchising from a variety of different perspectives. I interviewed franchisees, franchisors, business owners and the general public to gain their personal perspectives on franchising which included the good, the bad and the ugly. It was also heavily influenced by my extensive research into Transformational Leadership and the astounding results achieved by companies that followed this approach.

Franchisee Engagement is the Key

I have always believed franchising to be an excellent model for business growth but I equally knew that it had to change in order to bring it into line with current best business practices and thinking. Prior to my involvement with franchising, I had been part of the corporate world. Whilst enjoying a conversation with my business mentor, we suddenly came to the realisation that there was a huge crossover between employee engagement and franchisee engagement. This was the beginning of the creation of Transformative Franchising™. At its centre, it is about putting people before systems; trust; collaboration; integrity; respect; transparency and fairness. For example at Franchise Revolution™ we encourage our franchisors to call their franchisees 'franchise partners' to reflect the important placed on forming collaborative partnerships. Transformative Franchising™ is also about engaging the hearts and minds of franchise partners. Countless studies in business leadership and employee engagement, have demonstrated that Transformational Leadership can lead to highly sustainable performance, motivation and profit.

In conclusion, Transformative Franchising™ embeds the core values of mutual respect, trust, empowerment, collaboration, connectedness, transparency and fairness. It is a model that places huge emphasis on the importance of highly engaged franchise partners. It is a new paradigm that will redefine franchising, bringing it into line with the needs of 21st century businesses, and will showcase franchising to be the powerful growth strategy that it is.

Let us now look at the key differences between Transformative Franchising™ and conventional franchising.

TRANSFORMATIVE FRANCHISING™	CONVENTIONAL FRANCHISING
People are more important than systems and processes. Values such as transparency, trust and mutual respect are evident. There is a sense of purpose, a feeling of family	Contracts, agreements, systems, procedures and compliance take precedence
Franchisors engage with their franchise partners	Franchisors manage their franchisees
There is a shared mission and vision. Valued contribution from all parties is encouraged	Mission and values are decided by the franchisor. They are not always shared or endorsed by franchisees
Franchisors work collaboratively with franchise partners	Franchisors monitor franchisees for compliance
Franchisor/franchise partner relationship is interdependent. Collaboration and partnerships are valued	Collaboration is not always present. Franchisee and franchisor frequently work independently
Franchise partners are encouraged to share their initiative, ideas and previous experiences which are valued and utilized when appropriate	Innovations by franchisees are discouraged to maintain compliance and control
Shared experiences and collaboration is evident. Franchise partners are included in decision making for new systems, products or services	Top down approach is often adopted by franchisors when implementing new systems, products or services

Fair and balanced relationship for both parties	Power is weighted towards franchisor
Balanced fee structure for both parties. Win/win outcomes are sought	Excessive compensation for the franchisor
Franchise partners are highly motivated, committed and loyal to the franchisor and the brand	Franchisees feel disconnected to the franchisor
Franchise partners and franchisor go beyond their self-interests for the good of the network	Franchisee and franchisor serve their self-interest

N.B. I am fully aware there are many respected franchisors that fall to the left side of the table or somewhere between the two columns. I am not trying to discredit franchising in any way in its current form and am fully mindful that I have polarised the two categories. The purpose of this table is simply to illustrate how Transformative Franchising™ is a very different but powerful approach than its conventional counterpart, based on empirical studies on the huge benefits of transformational leadership in business.

I am also mindful that I needed to be a realist. I am aware that I am challenging the worldview of franchising and people may argue that there is nothing wrong with the current model. However, I also know through my extensive experiences and research that franchising can be a whole lot better for everyone involved and surely that can only be a positive thing.

THE INTERNATIONAL FRANCHISE ASSOCIATION IFA)

The International Franchise Association (IFA) was formed in the 1960s and is the world's oldest and largest organization representing franchising worldwide. The IFA's mission is to protect, enhance and promote franchising through government relations, public relations and educational programmes.

THE BRITISH FRANCHISE ASSOCIATION (BFA)

In the United Kingdom the BFA was set up in 1977 to improve franchising standards and to promote franchising. It encourages franchisors to become members in order to maintain ethical standards. The BFA's key publication the **Code of Ethics** governs franchisor membership.

Both of the above organisation offer many benefits to members which include:

- Booklets and publications
- Informative website
- Seminars for franchisors and franchisees
- Exhibitions
- Code of Ethics Standards
- Arbitration and mediation services
- Research

Transformative Franchising™ fully aligns itself to the ethos of both the IFA and the BFA. The key point of difference between Transformative Franchising™ and other franchise consultancies is the focus on the on-going relationship between the franchisor and its franchise partners. It is about franchise partner engagement, and putting people first. It is about collaboration; respect; trust

and integrity; fairness, and creating transformative partnerships that seek win/win outcomes.

CHAPTER THREE

Why is Transformative Franchising™ such a successful growth strategy?

Transformative Franchising™ is one of the most powerful growth strategies that can take your business to the next level. Few companies even consider franchising, and it is one of the best kept secrets in the business world. In this chapter, I am going to explain why franchising is a great alternative to more conventional growth strategies, and you will begin to see its extraordinary potential.

If you are in business, you will understand the impact of the economic downturn on either your own business, or on other businesses that have suffered. As stated earlier in the book, franchising continues to grow **despite** the current economic climate. This statement alone should have grabbed your attention. Why is this the case?

In order to grow a business there are several strategies that can be adopted. The strategy selected, will to some degree, depend on the amount of finances available to the business owner. Let's look at the most common growth strategies for small and medium sized businesses.

OPTION ONE

Increase your Productivity

Whilst this may seem an obvious statement it is surprising how many businesses do not have efficient systems and procedures in place which would enable them to sell more of their products or services and therefore increase profit. It may also be that the business owner will need to work harder as well as employ more staff to cope with the increased productivity. For some businesses, this strategy may be the answer as limited financial investment is required. Hard work and may be an upgrade in systems, as well as the costs of extra staff, is all that is often necessary for higher productivity.

OPTION TWO

Open another location

This is often the first strategy that businesses think of when planning to expand. Whilst this can often be the answer, there are several things to consider before moving ahead. How will you finance it? Is the new location similar in demographics to your existing location? How will you staff it? Do you want the responsibility of employing and managing large numbers of staff in various locations? Most importantly, does your existing company show a prolonged and sustainable bottom line? It can be costly and timely to open a new location and focus can be taken from your existing business in favour of the new "shiny" location at your cost!

OPTION THREE

Form Joint Ventures & Affiliate Schemes

This can be a lucrative growth strategy if you can find businesses that complement your own business. You will of course be expected to share the profit from sales and if this does not appeal to you then this it is not the right way to grow your business. You also need to be mindful of your brand image and ensure that your joint venture partners are a good "fit" for your product or service. Typically, you will source potential joint venture partners who will promote your product or service within their own business, often via their website, and share the profits from sales with you. In return, it is usual for you to do likewise with their product or service.

OPTION FOUR

Add more products/services

Are you able to diversify to offer more products or services? For example, if you are providing care services to older people, can you offer gardening services as well? If you are offering one to one services, can you develop your expertise into a DVD or online programme?

Adding new products and services is an expensive strategy in terms of cost and time. Many such initiatives fail as there is no market for the new products, or they are not compatible with the current brand and core products.

OPTION FIVE

Expand into other target markets

Consider your current product or service and then examine the market you are targeting. Perhaps there are other target markets that could also benefit from your product or service which may only need a slight amendment or re-brand in order to appeal to a different target market?

Expand Globally

With the advent of the internet, the world has become a very small marketplace. However, it is not just through internet sales that you can expand internationally. Many companies grow through establishing new outlets across the globe either from starting up themselves or through acquisitions. Again, your business needs to be in a strong financial place and you will require access to large financial resources in order to expand in this way.

This strategy requires a lot of market research and testing. If you want to go overseas this can be very expensive and take a long time to implement. There are also important currency and legal issues that you will need to consider carefully. For further information on expanding internationally please visit **http://www.ukti.gov.uk/home.html?guid=none**.

OPTION SIX

Establish new marketing channels

Most businesses nowadays have an internet presence but may be they are not maximising this opportunity. If you are not naturally a "techie" then source a company with expertise in this area. There are many companies that specialise in helping you to grow through maximising your website presence, as well as implementing a social media strategy to reach and engage with prospective franchise partners.

Depending on the type of product or service you are offering, you could also consider direct mail; print advertising; public relations; sponsorships etc.

OPTION SEVEN

Mergers and Acquisitions

Mergers

If you run a small independent company that is successful and maybe covers a specific geographical area or targets a specific market niche, larger companies who are looking to expand may well be interested in a merger with you. This option needs to be carefully considered as you will most likely lose control and direction of your business and find yourself submerged into a larger corporation.

Also, the best time to sell your business is when you are on a significant growth curve, and have several years of sustained profit. Most business owners try to sell when they are in a weaker, more vulnerable position and buyers take advantage of this.

Acquisitions

This is usually considered a suitable option for larger businesses that have the necessary financial resources, but it can be an efficient and fast route for expansion. Be aware that acquisitions are very costly not just in terms of finance, but also in time. You will need to dedicate yourself to finding suitable companies to buy, and spend months in negotiation, legal discussions and due diligence with a high risk of the deal collapsing. Moreover, many completed acquisitions provide a disappointing return. They require months, and sometimes years, of hard work to align the buyer and seller's products, systems, processes and, above all, people.

OPTION EIGHT

TRANSFORMATIVE FRANCHISING™

Franchising can incorporate **all** of the above growth strategies without you having to do anything extra, as you and your franchise partners naturally execute each option by:

- ✓ Boosting the productivity of current products and services
- ✓ Opening new locations
- ✓ Negating the need for you to create new products or services
- ✓ Providing new marketing channels
- ✓ Expanding into new markets
- ✓ Becoming your new joint venture partners
- ✓ Raising their own finances to start their franchise so you do not need to give away equity

However, if you want to leverage franchising as a growth strategy and maximise your profits even further, you can also utilise some of the options stated above. This will also help to attract franchise partners to your network more quickly as they will want to be part of a dynamic franchise. Let us look briefly at the options and how Transformative Franchising™ integrates with each one.

Option One – Increase your Productivity.

By default, if you decide that franchising is your chosen expansion route, then you will need to ensure that your systems and processes are running at maximum efficiency. They must be strong enough to be replicated by franchise partners without any difficulty. This in turn will produce a positive side effect of improving your current productivity as well as preparing you for franchise expansion.

Option Two – Open another Location

Franchising is ideal for expanding into new locations. The good news is that you do not need to finance this, as your franchise partners will be investing their own money into their new business venture. This option is extremely beneficial to your business, as your brand expands into new locations without the associated high costs and potential risk. Perhaps even more importantly, you do not have the liability of employing large numbers of staff and the associated costs. Franchise partners are liable for their own staff as well as your products or services.

Options Three to Five – Improving your Core Business

As part of your business expansion, as well as focusing on developing your franchise operation, it is also important to continue to enhance, improve and develop your core business so that both you and your franchise partners can benefit. If forming joint ventures fits with your business model, you will have a more attractive proposition to prospective joint venture partners as they will have access to all of your franchised locations. This in turn, benefits your franchise partners' profitability, as they will also enjoy the benefits of the joint venture partnership, which in turn increases your profitability. A clear win/win!

By adding more products or services, or expanding into new target markets and overseas, you will attract more franchise partners to your network as they will see the benefits of having multiple business opportunities that optimise their chances of success. Equally, this will not only ensure the success of your existing franchise partners but also your own core business, once again impacting positively on your bottom line.

Option Six – Establish New Market Channels

As stated earlier, as a franchisor, it will become increasingly important for you to continually develop your core business. This is good business practice. Being accountable to your franchise partners will support you in ensuring that you do not neglect this vital business growth component, and ensure your continued success. Part of this development should include a high quality, professional website as this will be your showcase to existing customers and franchise partners, as well as new prospective franchise partners. It may also be the case that your franchise partners do not have experience in this area, and as a forward thinking and innovative franchisor, you will gain a competitive advantage over other franchisors that may be competing in the same market as you are.

Option Seven – Mergers and Acquisitions

Whilst this can be a powerful growth strategy, it is extremely costly and also carries a higher risk as you will probably need to borrow large amounts of money or, give large percentages of your company away to venture capitalists.

Transformative Franchising™ allows you to expand wherever there is a franchise partner willing to join you in your venture. Although you may need to raise some finance, it will be significantly less than the amounts required for the above option and it certainly carries a much reduced risk. Additionally, you get to remain in control of your own company without having to give away large percentages or be "merged" into a larger corporation where you are likely to lose both your identity and control of your business.

CONCLUSION

I hope that you can begin to see the extraordinary potential of franchising, and how it is the optimal growth strategy for your business. By engaging a network of motivated franchise partners, you will be able to grow a highly profitable business incorporating all of the growth strategy options stated above in one go! Franchising is undoubtedly a cost effective, low risk, powerful method to leverage your business growth and profitability.

Transformative Franchising™ is the optimal franchising strategy for today's aspiring franchisor incorporating best current business practices and research. Over the following chapters I will demonstrate to you just how powerful this new franchise strategy actually is.

PART TWO

TRANSFORMATIVE FRANCHISING™ PRINCIPLES to take your business to the next level

In Part One, we established that franchising is a powerful way to leverage your business. We learned that conventional franchising is not working as well as it should, and has evolved very little over the last several decades. Conventional franchising emphasises systems and processes rather than people, synergy and growth. It has not reflected the vast changes in digital technology or the more empowered culture that drives business today. We have also learned that Transformative Franchising™ is without doubt, a superb and powerful way to leverage your business.

To recap on what we have learned so far:

- ✓ Franchising as a growth strategy, continues to increase despite the current economic climate
- ✓ Franchising in its current format is not working as well as it should

- ✓ Conventional franchising is focused on systems and procedures rather than people

- ✓ On-going franchisee engagement as opposed to monitoring and management, is the key to successful franchising

- ✓ Transformative Franchising™ is aligned to transformational leadership. Numerous empirical studies have emphatically and consistently demonstrated highly desired positive outcomes for employees and employers who have adopted this leadership style

✓ Transformative Franchising™ is a superior growth strategy and the optimal franchise system for success.

In Part Two, I will show you how you can take your business to the next level and grow a highly profitable and sustainable organisation by adopting and implementing the Transformative Franchising™ Principles. This will ensure that you stand out from the crowd and prospective franchise partners will want to partner with you rather than other competing franchisors, as they can see a compelling value proposition based on trust and collaboration that seeks to prosper both parties.

CHAPTER FOUR

How is Transformative Franchising™ different?

In this chapter we will look at how Transformative Franchising™ is superior to conventional franchising by examining some key differences.

My Story

Looking back over my working life I realise now that I have always been entrepreneurial but had not realised it! I remember one of my first ideas back in the 1980s was to launch a calorie counted sandwich and snack range. I was calorie counting (as was virtually everyone I knew!). At that time there was nowhere to purchase calorie counted sandwiches or lunch time snacks and this became my big idea. However, I simply had no idea as to how to go about launching such a business. The internet did not exist at that time and there were no business groups, mentors or business advisors on hand to help me that I was aware of. Nowadays, one click on the internet can produce a huge array of free information. Needless to say it remained a big idea in my head. Interestingly, about two years later, Boots the Chemist launched the first ever range of calorie counted Sandwiches, followed shortly by the supermarkets. The rest is history.

I began researching franchise opportunities at the end of the 1990s. Again, I really did not have much of an idea of how to start my own independent business, so felt that franchising could be the answer. Over the following decade I investigated a plethora of different franchise opportunities – some were good, some were average and some were really bad. The interesting point that I want to make here, is that the only reason I did not buy a franchise was because of what I believed to be **a complete imbalance of power between the franchisor and franchisee.** It seemed that whichever way I turned, the franchisor had the "upper hand". This view was further endorsed by my friends and colleagues who also believed that is was only the franchisor that benefited.

During this time I was fully employed but desperate to run my own business. I had tried network marketing and other "business opportunities" but none met with my expectations. In 2002 I launched a colour business which supported people to select the right colours for their homes from a deeper emotional level. I was ahead of my times and only enjoyed limited success. A couple of years after I had closed this business, Crown started to promote their colour schemes in a very similar way to me, and was a great success. In 2005 I started my second business on a part time basis, running pamper parties for girls between 4 to 14 years of age. This was very successful and I decided to invite franchise partners to share my vision. It was run as a collaborative partnership between me and my franchise partners. I implemented all of the positive practices that I had learned from the franchise model and avoided those that I felt were unfair or treated my franchise partners as employees. At this time, I did not realise that this was the beginning of Transformative Franchising™. A couple of years later, my personal circumstances took me to Spain. I continued the business briefly during this time but decided to sell the business to my franchise partners to continue, as I felt I could not offer my full support.

Whilst in Spain, I continued to research into franchise opportunities, but again the results were the same as my previous endeavours and needless to say I did not buy into one. My family and I returned to the United Kingdom in 2007. At this point, I did not want to return to employment but needed to ensure that any business venture I embarked upon would enjoy maximum success. The answer – buy a franchise! I eventually bought into a start-up franchise at the end of 2007 which satisfied my entrepreneurial nature as I would be part of its growth. The years spent as a franchisee from the "inside-out" served me extremely well in preparation for Franchise Revolution™ and Transformative Franchising™. I was in the privileged position to view franchising from both sides of the equation. It was from these experiences that I learned what really worked well and what did not and the importance of engaging franchise partners rather than monitoring and controlling them.

Why Transformative Franchising™ is the Future?

As we have learned previously, there has been extensive research into the massive benefits of Transformational Leadership which seeks to build trust, kindness, integrity, engagement and empowerment with its employees. (See Transformational Leadership, Riggio & Bass, 2006; Transformational Leadership, Dr E J Shelton, 2012; Lead from the Heart, M.C.Crowley, 2011.) We have also learned that these values lead to increased motivation, loyalty and ultimately profitable outcomes and a sustainable business. Now, this model of Transformational Leadership has been translated into franchising, to enable you to build a successful franchise business based on these principles.

As well as the principles of transformational leadership, conventional franchising can often lag behind in harnessing the power of modern technology. Franchise Revolution™ practices what it preaches by integrating modern technology into its very heart. Franchisors and businesses who wish to franchise are offered both online and offline franchise consultancy programmes. We know that social media is paramount to any business and again, this is embedded throughout Franchise Revolution™ and Transformative Franchising™.

The Transformative Franchising™ Vision

THE 6 KEY PRINCIPLES OF TRANSFORMATIVE FRANCHISING™

- Creates a Compelling Shared Vision
- Puts People First
- Recognises that Engagement is the Key
- Creates Win/Win Outcomes
- Leverages Digital Technology
- Encourages Life Long Learning

Transformative Franchising takes franchising to the next level, and embraces important developments in business practice, leadership, technology and, above all, relationships. It represents a new generation of thinking about Partnerships, and specifically the relationship between Franchisor and Franchise Partner. It also offers the promise of taking your own business to the next level of growth and profitability.

So let's look in more detail at the six key principles of Transformative Franchising™.

The Characteristics of the Transformative Franchisor

1 Creates a Compelling Shared Vision

The Transformative Franchisor inspires, motivates and empowers franchise partners to share their vision working together as a team. Franchisors and franchise partners share and utilise past experiences, skills and innovations to make the vision a reality. When both partners share a compelling vision, they work together with much greater passion, clarity, motivation and energy. This in turn boosts productivity and work satisfaction, which is a powerful combination for sustained high performance.

2 Puts People First

Transformative Franchising™ understands that people are more important than systems and processes. The franchisor values franchise partners' ideas, views, and contributions. collaboration, mutual respect, integrity and trust are embedded throughout the organisation. Many managers and executives talk about putting people first, but do not match their words with action. The Transformative Franchisor is committed to this principle, and this is their core value. Every element of their business is built around this core value, and you can see it in action in every activity.

3 Recognises that Franchise Partner Engagement is Paramount.

The Transformative Franchisor recognises the importance of franchise partner engagement, as opposed to conventional franchisee monitoring and compliance. Partnerships collapse if there is a hint of deceit.

Franchise partner engagement commences at the very first connection, through to termination of the franchise agreement. It is important that franchisors demonstrate their commitment to Transformative Franchising™ by collaborating and communicating with prospective franchise partners even before they sign the franchise agreement and become part of the franchise network. For example, the franchisor may be able to demonstrate collaboration through a recent Operations Manual update that has evidence of franchise partner collaboration. Transformative Franchising™ also encourages the franchisor to expose the prospective franchise partner to as much of the business as possible, prior to signing the franchise agreement. This allows the franchise partner to gain a more in depth understanding of what is actually involved in running the franchise, so that when they eventually commence trading there will hopefully be no hidden surprises! This also helps to augment the franchise relationship from the outset.

Transformative Franchising™ relationships are built around a culture of integrity and trust. This is a long-term commitment and leads to greater understanding, and also sustained higher performance as the franchise partner feels more positive and passionate about the partnership.

4 Ensures that Franchise Partnerships are Fair, Equitable and Balanced.

A culture of win/win is evident in the legal agreements and the franchise relationships. The Transformative Franchisor recognises and celebrates franchise partners' accomplishments and provides opportunities for personal development and growth. Support is tailored to the franchise partners' needs rather than used as a means to monitor for compliance. Support is collaborative rather than dictatorial. A culture of trust, respect and transparency prevails.

5 Leverages Digital Technology

The Transformative Franchisor leverages the full power of the internet, social media and mobile technology to support franchise partners. They acknowledge that technology is transforming the way business is conducted, and ensure that their franchise provides cutting-edge tools and techniques to take advantage of these developments.

6 Supports Lifelong Learning

The Transformative Franchisor is committed to lifelong learning to stay ahead of the   competition, and adapt to the continuous changes in the business world. Nothing stands still and the Transformative Franchisor takes a dynamic approach providing high level training and coaching, to ensure that their partners have the most appropriate knowledge and skills to achieve sustained high performance. This includes both offline training and online E-Learning.

CHAPTER FIVE

The Transformative Franchising™ Development Model

The following chapters will show you how you can take your business to the next level by adopting Transformative Franchising™. Whilst Transformative Franchising™ is primarily aimed at putting people first, there are still essential stages that need to be completed in order to develop a successful franchise. I will examine each stage of the process and suggest ways in which you can stand above your competitors by integrating Transformative Franchising™ throughout each stage.

STAGE ONE

First Things First

In the UK there are no legal formalities required in order to franchise your business. However, as you will be inviting franchise partners to invest money and time into your franchise system, it is unethical and very poor practice to do so without first carrying out your own due diligence, research and planning. The first vital step is to carry out an assessment to ascertain whether a) your business can be franchised, and b) you are ready to franchise.

Below is a short example of the type of questions you need to be able to answer. **You can download a free copy of the full version at http://franchiserevolution.co.uk/resources**

- ✓ Do you have a profitable trading position?
- ✓ Have you run a pilot franchise?
- ✓ Can your business be replicated?

- ✓ Can you teach others to replicate your business relatively easily?
- ✓ Do you own the intellectual property rights of your business?
- ✓ Can the business operate profitably in different geographical and demographic areas?
- ✓ Are you really ready to move to the next level of your business growth?

A final but important question to consider. Do **you** want to focus on the franchise development personally, or do you want to employ a franchise manager or engage a professional franchise consultancy to manage and oversee this part of your business allowing you to continue to focus on your core business? Essentially, when you become a franchisor, you are starting a new and different business. (Either way you will need the support of a professional franchise consultancy such as Franchise Revolution™, to guide you through the process and to help you avoid making expensive mistakes).

The above questions are by no means exhaustive and the more you can answer in the affirmative, the more success you are likely to enjoy. If you have answered 'no' to a lot of the questions, please do not be disheartened. A reputable franchise consultant such as Franchise Revolution™ will be able to assess the viability of franchising your business and will be able to support you in preparing your business for franchising.

The Big Question - Pilot or not to Pilot?

Whilst running a pilot franchise is preferable, it is by no means essential. The main benefit to running a pilot office is to demonstrate that you can answer the questions above - that your business can be replicated and profitable for franchise partners. If, for example, you run an estate agency, it is fair to say that this model will work in most areas as there are estate agencies everywhere. If you run a bespoke business that is unique to your area, I would suggest that you run a pilot franchise elsewhere in a different location and with different demographics to ensure its success. This will be important to your franchise partners, as they will need to be sure that your business model works in other areas. It would be unethical of you to do this without first checking the viability of the business.

Another benefit to running a pilot franchise is to transfer the practical know how, into an Operations Manual. Most things that happen in the pilot operation will happen in your franchise partners' businesses and so it is vital that you can capture this information into a comprehensive Operations Manual. You will also discover other factors when operating a pilot that you may not have experienced in your core business.

STAGE TWO

PRE-LAUNCH

> *"If you fail to plan, you plan to fail"*   (Harvey MacKay)

You are now happy that your business can be franchised. The following section will support you in the practical applications necessary to prepare your business ready for its franchise launch, the Transformative Franchising™ way.

I. BUSINESS PLAN

For any new business venture planning is essential and writing a business plan is the first step. It is also a requirement if you need to raise finance from a bank or venture capitalist. A business plan helps you to:

- clarify your franchise idea
- spot potential problems
- set out your goals
- measure your progress

The business plan should be comprehensive and include all of the key elements. Below, is a framework for a very simplified business plan. Please visit **http://www.entrepreneur.com/formnet/form/459** for a wide selection of business templates and tools.

Executive Summary

I suggest you write this last! Once you have completed the other sections, the Executive Summary will be a concise overview of your franchise business plan highlighting the key points that you have made. You need to engage the attention of your target reader straight away, who may well be an investor or financial lender, so it is vital that you get this right!

Business Summary

This section is an overview of your business and includes your overall vision and what you expect to achieve. Remember that you need to create a compelling vision that can be shared by others. It should include:

- who you are
- what you do
- Your unique selling points (USP)
- your experience
- when your company was founded
- who are the owners/directors
- your vision and goals
- your reason for choosing franchising as a growth strategy
- your trading history
- a brief profile of your preferred franchise partners

Products and Services

Describe the products or services that your business offers and how you aim to replicate these by engaging franchise partners. You may want to include the current success of your business and how you believe your franchise partners can benefit from this.

Market and Competitor Analysis Summary

Describe the type of business sector you are in and show that it has longevity. This is important as franchise partners will need to feel confident that they are able to make a return on their investment during the term of the franchise agreement. Also demonstrate that you have undertaken comprehensive competitor research to evidence that there is room for your franchise partners to operate in your particular market.

Strategy and Implementation Summary

What is your business USP? What is your value proposition? What is your brand position in the market sector you are in? Why do customers buy from you? Why will franchise partners want to join you? How will you ensure that your product or service will continue to be attractive to both existing and new customers for the benefit of your franchise partners? How will you evaluate the success of your business? You may want to include franchise partner recruitment plans here.

Management Summary

Describe how the franchise operation will be staffed including roles and responsibilities. You may want to include the engagement of a franchise consultant. Explain your role within the franchise element of the business. Who will recruit your franchise partners?

Financial Plan

This section will include your profit and loss and cash flow forecasts; break even analysis; and franchise partner recruitment projections. You may also want to include your last three years business trading reports here. It is important to record the assumptions you are making in regards to the projections you have made i.e. to recruit one franchise partner every other month.

2. TRADEMARKS AND INTELLECTUAL PROPERTY

One of the key components to franchising is the licensing of your intellectual property to your franchise partners. This can include the name, logo, tag or strap line. Franchise partners are buying into your brand and it is essential that this is protected. It is therefore imperative that you apply for a trademark if you have not already done so. This can be done relatively easily either through a lawyer, specialist trademark registration company or you can do this yourself, online at the government site for the Intellectual Property Office, **http://www.ipo.gov.uk/** , if you are in the UK or **http://www.uspto.gov/** for the US and **http://www.wipo.int/madrid/en/** for a wider country coverage. I would also suggest that you allow at least six months for this to be processed if possible. Finally, if your trademark is already registered to your core company, then you will need to arrange to license it to your franchise company if this is a separate entity.

3. FRANCHISE DEVELOPMENT PLAN

Prior to recruiting your first franchise partners, you will need to ensure that you have everything in place for a smooth and seamless transition. There are several documents and systems that you will need to develop as part of your franchise portfolio. We will look at each of them individually.

Franchise Central Office

This is the office that will be dedicated to the franchise part of your business. As part of your business plan, you will have included a franchise central office staff plan which illustrates at which points you will need to recruit staff to support your franchise partners as the network develops. The number of central office staff that you initially employ will be dependent on how much, or how little, you want to be involved with the franchise development. For example, if you choose to conduct your franchise partner recruitment in-house, it is usual to employ a **Franchise Recruitment Manager** although in the early stages you may prefer to do this yourself. This is an extremely important, but time consuming role and whilst it necessary for you to be involved with the recruitment process at some level, you will need someone to oversee the day to day duties such as handling enquiries, marketing, interviews and so on.

You should also be considering who will train and support your initial franchise partners, and you may well be the best person for this at this stage. This will assist you in knowing what is required, when you come to recruit for these positions. Both recruitment and trainer roles are again of vital importance at the early stages, and throughout the lifetime of the franchise. Finally, it is also important to ensure that all of your franchise central office staff are made aware of the ethos of Transformative Franchising™ to encourage everyone to work towards the same outcomes.

FRANCHISE CENTRAL OFFICE - INTERNAL SYSTEMS AND PROCESSES

It will be assumed that you already have a successful business, and that you are considering Transformative franchising™ to leverage your growth. You will most likely already have some systems and processes in place for your core business, but these may not be suitable for a franchise operation. You will need to ensure that your systems have the capability to support a network of franchise partners throughout the country, or internationally. This may mean that you will need to upgrade, or install new systems. Consider how your customer data is stored? Do you intend to keep customer data at the central office only, or will franchise partners store this data? Perhaps you will have a system that both you and your franchise partners can access? With the introduction of the Cloud, it is much easier to overcome these problems. You will also need to be mindful that your franchise partners will need to comply with the Data Protection Act.

FRANCHISE OPERATING SYSTEMS

These are the operating systems that form the key part of your franchise offering. They need to be relatively easy to follow as well as effective and efficient. For example, if you run a product business your operating system should consider:

- Will you have a central website?
- Is there a central telephone ordering line or do franchise partners have their own telephone ordering line?
- How will stock be ordered?
- How will customer's orders be processed?
- How will the products be delivered?
- How will customer's pay – to the franchise partner or directly to central office?
- Where will stock be stored?

This is only a small example. However, as you are already running a business, it should be relatively easy to create these systems.

FRANCHISE PARTNER TERRITORY

Most franchise partners will expect an exclusive territory and may not consider your franchise offering if this is not the case. This is quite a complex area and much thought needs to be put into this. For example, you may need to consider what happens if one of your franchise partners is not working their whole territory effectively. If the franchise agreement offers an exclusive territory, there needs to be protection for you within the agreement. Problems of this nature are less likely to occur if you are adopting the Transformative Franchising™ model.

The territories need to be divided in such a way that all franchise partners have an equal chance of success. For example, if you currently run a care services business you will need to ensure that every territory has a similar number of residents within your target market, to ensure you can replicate your current business's success. If you run a grass cutting service, there is no use in offering a large territory that primarily consists of flats, or very small gardens!

TRANSFORMATIVE FRANCHISING™ PROSPECTUS (BROCHURE)

This is your "sales brochure" and is therefore of the utmost importance, as it is often the first material a prospective franchise partner will receive from you. First impressions are very important, and your brochure should reflect the business opportunity. For example, if you are offering an executive or professional type of franchise opportunity, then your prospectus should reflect this by using high quality gloss paper, eye catching graphics, suitable photos, and so on.

It is important to note that this document can also be used in litigation if it was believed that you had deliberately misled prospective franchise partners into buying your franchise based on stated projected earnings that you were aware were over-inflated and not likely to be achieved. For example, if you make claims that a franchise partner can earn £100k in the second year by following your systems, and they fall significantly short of this amount, you could be accused of "misrepresentation" if the franchise partner should resort to litigation. **Trust, honesty and transparency are key principles in Transformative Franchising™** and the franchise prospectus should embed these values to protect both franchisor and franchise partners throughout the term of the franchise agreement.

So, what should be included in your franchise prospectus? In a nutshell, it is a brief overview of the franchise package offering, with enough information to enable a prospective franchise partner to want to make a decision to request further information. It should also be able to deter people who may not be suitable. For example, the earning potential may not be sufficient, or they do not have the required finances.

Examples of suggested franchise prospectus key headings are:
- Contents Page
- Overview
- The Business Opportunity (about your business, what is the opp?)
- Why choose franchising?

- Training and Support
- Earning Potential
- Franchise Package
- Next Steps (call to action)
- Enquiry Form

Let us look briefly at each heading.

1. **Contents**

   A contents page with page numbers to support easy navigation of the prospectus

2. **Overview**

   This section should include an overview of both your current business and the franchise opportunity of the same. It should illustrate the key benefits a person would gain by becoming one of your franchise partners and a brief suggested profile of the type of person that would thrive by owning one of your franchises.

3. **The Business Opportunity**

   This is the section where you can really showcase your business. You need to demonstrate why franchise partners should choose you over other similar franchises - that it is a proven business formula for success with strong branding; that you can assist with raising finance; the huge benefits of being part of a team and of course that you endorse Transformative Franchising™.

(**Visit http://franchiserevolution.co.uk/resources** for an online franchise partner promotional leaflet on the benefits of Transformative Franchising™ which you can give to your prospective franchise partners.)

4. The Market Opportunity

Ideally this needs to be your business story, and the success you have achieved to date. It needs to illustrate the potential for franchise partners to invest, and develop their own successful businesses based on your proven business format. It can also include an overview of the market you are operating in (if applicable).

5. Why Choose Transformative™ Franchising?

It is important to advise the prospective franchise partner of the benefits of Transformative Franchising™, as opposed to setting up on their own independently.   As well as highlighting the "softer" benefits such as collaboration, trust and respect, you can also include statistics on the success of operating a franchise as opposed to going it alone, or being part of a team for example. It may be at this stage; prospective franchise partners have read your business opportunity with great interest and are now pondering whether they can go it alone? Remember to remain open, honest and transparent in your communication, as it is no use in recruiting a franchise partner that is more suitable being independent.

6. Training and Support

Following on from the previous statement, franchise partners will want to know what they will get as part of the package before proceeding any further. Training and support needs to be clearly stated and attractive to a prospective franchise partner as this may be the decisive factor in selecting your franchise. You should include details of the initial training as well as ongoing training and support and if applicable, an annual conference and regional meetings. You could even give them a schedule of exactly what will happen when they join, so they can visualize themselves owning the franchise and experiencing your training and support.

7. Earning Potential

It is usual practice to forecast the first three years of projected profit to enable a prospective franchise partner to ascertain whether this is sufficient for their needs. A word of caution here! Whilst you need to attract franchise partners into the network, you need to be honest and transparent with your predicted earnings. As mentioned earlier, any representations that you make in your literature can be used against you if it is felt that you deliberately misled your franchise partners. That aside, Transformative Franchising™ does not endorse advertising misleading statements and profit forecasts, as this is fundamentally against its core principles.

8. Franchise Package

This section outlines the complete franchise package. It should include:
- The initial franchise fee and when it is payable
- On-going franchise management fees
- Marketing fees (if applicable)
- The brief terms of the franchise
- Territories and whether they are exclusive

- Use of the intellectual property
- Training & support the Transformative Franchising™ way
- Operations Manual
- Full details of what is included in the startup package. For example, letterheads, website, brochures, initial marketing, lead generation etc.

9. NEXT STEPS

It is vital that you make it easy for a prospective franchise partner to contact you by phone and email. I would suggest that you have a "call to action" on each page of the prospectus. You may also want to include an enquiry form as part of the "call to action".

Electronic or Hard Copy Brochure?

This is ultimately down to you. In today's technological society, electronic brochures are perfectly acceptable, and also much cheaper! However, I would suggest that you also keep a stock of hard copy brochures for franchise exhibitions and for those people that request one. Some people may still prefer a brochure over an electronic version, that they can touch and that also reflects the quality of the franchise offering. I know I do!

4   LEGAL ESSENTIALS

There are a number of legal documents that you will need to be aware of. Please do not be put off by this as they are there to protect both you and your franchise partners. Your franchise consultant should be able to discuss these in more detail as well as the importance of engaging a specialist franchise lawyer.

Let us look briefly at the key legal documents.

1. Non-Disclosure Agreement

This is simply to protect you from a prospective franchise partner copying your ideas. As part of your recruitment process, you will need to disclose a certain amount of confidential information in order to give the prospective franchise partner an understanding of the business. An NDA is usually no more than a couple of pages and should be fair to both parties. I would strongly suggest that you send this out prior to the meeting, to allow the franchise partner time to read through and agree with its contents. They can then sign it and either return it by post or bring it to the meeting. It should be fair and not too onerous and should only refer to information that is not available in the public domain. It is common practice for the "non-compete" clause to last a maximum of 12 months and no longer. I have seen many NDA's during my time researching various franchises. Some were presented to me on the day of the meeting, which caused me to feel under pressure to sign. This was not a good start to the meeting! Often they were too onerous i.e. two years non-compete clauses. Sometimes the information is already available in the public domain if you researched it, or, the "confidential" operating system is just common sense and something you may well have considered doing yourself.

2. Deposit Agreement

Following the meeting, or meetings with prospective franchise partners, you and your franchise partner may wish to proceed to the next stage of the recruitment process. This is often to reserve a territory allowing the prospective franchise partner time to research the opportunity and carry out due diligence. It is common practice for a franchisor to ask for a deposit at this stage. This will also demonstrate the franchise partner's commitment. The Deposit Agreement needs to be signed by both franchisor and the franchise partner, stating the amount of the deposit, and the terms and conditions i.e. is the deposit refundable? And can this be offset against the franchise fee should they proceed?

3. Transformative Franchising™ Franchise Agreement

This is **the most important legal document in the whole process**. This is the contract that binds you, the franchisor, with your franchise partners. The franchise agreement is also often the reason why franchise partners bail out at the last minute if they have not had sight of this earlier on in the recruitment journey. I would strongly suggest that you offer your franchise agreement to your prospective franchise partners, for early perusal. They can then ask questions much earlier on in the process and save both of you a considerable amount of wasted time and effort. As I mentioned earlier on, the franchise agreement always needs to be biased towards the franchisor as you need to be protected. However, I would also strongly state here, that many franchise agreements are far too one-sided and in the worst case scenarios they could be described as exploitative! I have seen many. Some were good and some were very, very bad. It is not the remit of this E-book to go into great detail and I would strongly urge you to find a reputable franchise lawyer who can write this for you.

One important note to make is that franchising requires that all franchise partners work to the same agreement. Franchising's strength is its consistency. However, there is an opportunity to negotiate certain unsatisfactory clauses within the franchise agreement, in the form of a *Side Letter.* The side letter needs to be written by a franchise lawyer as it forms part of the Franchise Agreement and it is good practice to include the side letter as part of the initial franchise agreement, and not added in later.

As I mentioned earlier on, the franchise agreement is nearly always written in favour of the franchisor in order to protect your interests. This can be unsettling to franchise partners that may not have seen a franchise agreement before. However, the agreement also needs to protect your franchise partner's interests should things go wrong. All franchise agreements carry standard clauses but the content within these clauses, vary from franchisor to franchisor. It is these clauses that we are going to focus on by suggesting ways in which you can integrate Transformative Franchising™ into the franchise agreement.

Key clauses
- Franchisor's obligations
- Franchisee's obligations
- Franchisee's right to renew
- Sale of the business
- Death or incapacity of the franchisee
- Franchise fees
- Termination of the agreement and non-compete clauses

We will now briefly look at each clause and I will highlight ways that Transformative Franchising™ can be integrated into the agreement to create a win/win partnership.

TRANSFORMATIVE FRANCHIISING™ AGREEMENT	CONVENTIONAL FRANCHISE AGREEMENT
The Franchise Agreement is written in plain English and avoids legal jargon. There is an explanatory supplement which states the reasons why certain clauses are in place.	**The Franchise Agreement** is loaded with legal jargon. There is no explanatory supplement. The agreement is onerous with numerous excessive pages.
Franchisors Obligations - ensures that obligations are fair and supports both parties. Obligations reflect partnerships, collaboration, trust and transparency.	**Franchisors Obligations** –ensures that franchisors have excessive control.
Franchise Partners' Obligations – ensures that these are not too onerous for the franchise partner. That they reflect a fair and balanced approach whilst allowing protection for the franchisor when appropriate.	**Franchisee Obligations** – lengthy list of obligations, sometimes onerous and unnecessary. Exhibits evidence of compliance and control rather than collaboration and trust.
Right to Renew – offers franchise partners the right to renew without onerous restrictions or unfair renewal charges. Based on fairness, and respects the franchise partner's achievements.	**Right to Renew** – can be variable. Some franchisors ask for more money which is often a percentage of the then current initial franchise fee, despite earning fees from franchisees over the term. Others place onerous conditions. In rare cases, there may not be a right to renew!

Sale of Business – Recognises that franchise partners want to earn a fair return on their investment and therefore excessive fees are not charged. Also acknowledges those franchise partners that have built very successful businesses and does not penalise them by charging a percentage of sale price. Works alongside franchise partners to find the right purchaser and is fair in approving new franchise partners. Works collaboratively, ensuring a smooth sale.	**Sale of Business** – A large majority of franchisors charge 10% plus 10% of the purchase price, which represents commission and training respectively. This is applicable whether the purchaser is either a new or an existing franchisee who wants to expand. The more the business is worth, the more commission is paid. This is not reflective of the amount of work required from the franchisor and penalises successful franchisees that have built a large and profitable business, and paid significant management fees throughout the term.
Franchise Management Fees – Transformative Franchising™ understands that management fees need to be fair to both parties. Recognises that franchise partners need to make a healthy profit too. Recognition is awarded to franchise partners that perform well. This maybe discounts or a capped fee. Franchise partners feel that they are receiving very good value from the franchisor in terms of on-going training and support.	**Franchise Management Fees** – usually based on turnover which may be excessive compared to gross profit. Sometimes charged regardless of whether or not a franchisee has made a sale in that period. Often does not reward more successful franchisees who achieve high turnovers. Does not always represent value for money. Support and training are not always of a high enough standard to warrant the excessive management fees charged.
Termination of Agreement – Transformative Franchising™ is based on principles of trust, mutual respect and collaboration. Termination of	**Termination of Agreement** – Franchisees who are not compliant; or who have disregarded the franchise agreement may be at risk of

the agreement from either side is therefore far less likely to occur. When it is unavoidable, the franchisor works alongside the franchise partner in a collaborative and supportive way to resolve issues and achieve a win/win outcome whenever possible.	having their franchise terminated. The franchise agreement is heavily weighted in favour of the franchisor which can cause conflict between both parties. Legal intervention is frequently required.
Post Termination – Non-compete clauses are reasonable and fair and protect both franchisor and franchise partners.	**Post Termination –** Non-compete clauses can be onerous and heavily weighted in favour of the franchisor.

N.B. As per my note under the previous table, I am aware that a lot of franchisors already adopt a Transformative Franchising™ approach and not all are representative of the comments made under conventional franchising. Transformative Franchising™ is fully aligned to the IFA and the BFA Code of Ethics, but unfortunately not all franchisors take heed of this very important document.

Other Legal Documents

The legal documents mentioned so far are only part of the portfolio that may be required in order to run a professional franchise. Others include lease agreements; software agreements; intellectual property rights; and telephone transfer agreement.

5   TRANSFORMATIVE FRANCHISING™ OPERATIONS MANUAL

The Operations Manual is one of the most critical documents that you will require in order to achieve a successful franchise operation. This is the manual that will detail to the franchise partner, how the franchised business will operate. If you have already run a pilot franchise office, then this may be easier to write as you will already have previous experience. If not, you will need to write your Operations Manual based on your current business.

The Operations Manual needs to detail every part of your business ensuring there is no ambiguity. This is for the benefit of the whole network as all franchise partners need to be working together towards a shared vision. Each Operation Manual will be different dependent on the type of business you are operating. However, there are certain key headings that are applicable to most businesses.

1   INTRODUCTION

(a) A brief summary of the franchise business.

(b) What the franchise partner is expected to do in terms of commitment.

(c) What the franchisor will provide.

(d) A summary of the existing franchise network.

(e) Business philosophy, mission statement and core organisation values

2   SYSTEM

A detailed description of the system and its constituent parts.

3   OPERATING METHODS (Example)

(a) Equipment

(b) How to operate the equipment

(c) Stock requirement

(d) Hardware/Software

(e) Vehicle requirements

4   OPERATING INSTRUCTIONS (Example)

(a) All standard letters and forms

(b) Record keeping

(c) Uniforms,

(d) Training

(e) Opening times

(f) Advertising and marketing

5   OUTLET

The premises required and any branded fittings required

6   LEGISLATION

Any relevant legislation such as industry specific, employment

7   FRANCHISOR'S DIRECTORY

Central office staff and job descriptions, organisation chart

8   USEFUL TELEPHONE NUMBERS AND CONTACT DETAILS

I would suggest that you produce the Operations Manual online in a protected format to ensure that it cannot be printed, downloaded or copied in any way as well as ensuring that you have sufficient internet firewall protection. It is also a good idea to produce an interactive and searchable manual encouraging franchise partners to share their experiences and make comments.   This facilitates franchise partner engagement by encouraging collaboration and connectedness. An online operations manual also enables you to make very quick amendments as well as saving you time and money in printing and postage costs.

6   INITIAL TRAINING

Developing a successful franchise operation depends on the ability of all of the franchise partners to be competent to replicate the business model. Training is therefore fundamental to achieving success for all parties.

Some businesses are relatively straightforward to replicate, and it will take less time to train new franchise partners.   Others are more complex, and consequently the training will need to be more detailed and probably be conducted over a longer period of time. It is difficult to say how long training should last but as a ball park figure, I would suggest a minimum of five days for a more straight forward business and anything upwards. for more complex businesses. For example, a McDonald's franchisee is required to work on the counter for around nine months before getting involved in the management side!

Training will be the first real experience a new franchise partner will have of your business and will make a lasting impression. It is therefore imperative that you get this right from the start. Before we even consider the training content, you need to ensure that this is delivered by someone who is competent to do so and who is passionate about your business. There is nothing worse than a disorganised or disinterested trainer.

Firstly, you will need to identify the core skills needed in order to run a successful franchised business. You will know what these are from the experiences of running either your own business or your pilot operation, if you have run one. The ability to train your franchise partners to replicate your business is vital to the on-going success of everyone.

The content should be comprehensive and include everything that a new franchise partner needs in order to set up their business. Obviously, they will not remember everything and this is where the Operations Manual and the on-going support come into their own. Some franchisors work through the Operations Manual to ensure that everything is covered. Whilst this is useful, please do ensure that you vary the way the training is delivered in order to keep franchise partners' attention and motivation. For example, include role play, E-Learning; hands-on training (if possible) and ensure that it is interactive and supportive.

It is usual practice to divide the training into two parts:

i)   How to run a business. This will include all aspects of running a business such as:

- Accounts, including cash flow and credit control
- VAT
- Forming a company
- Employing staff
- Health & safety
- Industry specific requirements
- Data Protection

- Marketing
- Franchise fees
- IT

ii)   This section will cover everything relating to the particular product or service on offer. For example if the business was a lawn cutting service you would include:

- How to obtain a CRB
- More specific health & safety
- How to market the business
- How to sell the service
- How to handle enquiries
- How to plan your visits
- How to deliver the service
- How to take payments
- What equipment you will require
- Customer service

Most franchisors will conduct a competency test at the end of the training to ensure that the franchise partner is competent and confident to set up and run their new business. This is an opportunity for both parties to highlight any potential problem areas. If this is conducted in the right manner, a franchise partner will view it as a benefit, rather than an obstacle.

It is very important to ensure that all franchise partners are trained in the same way and cover the same content. Whilst some may be more experienced in business matters and others in the sector you are in, it is vital that you cover everything to avoid any potential problems arising later on in the partnership.

7 TRANSFORMATIVE FRANCHISING™ BUSINESS PLAN TEMPLATE FOR FRANCHISE PARTNERS

Many of your franchise partners may not have run a business previously and will be relying on you for support. They may also need to raise finance and a business plan will be required. It is good practice to design a template business plan for franchise partners to complete. The plan should incorporate both narrative as well as financial forecasts. **You can download a copy at http://franchiserevolution.co.uk/resources.** It is important to allow the franchise partner to make their own financial projections based on their research. Also, ensure that any financial forecasts you submit to a prospective franchise partner, are conservative and include all costs. Franchise Partners may be inexperienced and not able to achieve the same financial results as you have. As much as you want to make the business proposition attractive, it is unethical at best and against the ethos of Transformative Franchising™ and the IFA and BFA Code of Ethics, to offer an over inflated forecast. This will surely lead to problems later on when franchise partners realise that they are unable to achieve the profits they were expecting. This could also result in a misrepresentation legal claim against you. Definitely something to be avoided!

CHAPTER SIX

Launch

You are now finally ready to launch your franchise and take your business to the next level. The first step that you need to take is a step backwards! It is very tempting to jump in and recruit the first franchise partner that comes to you waving a cheque. I strongly suggest that you write a Franchise Recruitment Marketing Strategy if you have not already done so. This will help focus your attention back to the task in hand and is not as onerous as it may sound. It will also save you from potential problems later on. **One of the biggest mistakes new franchisors make is recruiting the wrong franchise partners.** So it is critical that you prevent this from happening by developing a clear, precise strategy for qualifying and recruiting the right people. The strategy should include:

a) Franchise Partner Profile
b) Recruitment Marketing Plan
c) Evaluating the Marketing Plan
d) Franchise Partner Recruitment Process Flow Chart

STEP ONE

Transformative Franchising™ Franchise Partner Profile.

Before you can start to advertise for franchise partners, you need to have a clear idea of the type of partner you are looking for! What type of skills, qualities, attributes or qualifications will they need? Do you require them to have previous experience of your business sector or would you prefer them to have none? Do they have, or will they be able to raise the necessary finance?

Are you offering a lifestyle business or a business that can be sold on later for a good profit? Is the income potential high enough for your franchise partners?

Whichever market you are in, you will need to consider the following:

- ✓ Cost of the franchise including working capital
- ✓ Expected income levels for the franchise partner
- ✓ Full or part time
- ✓ Type of franchised environment i.e. office or van based?
- ✓ What role will franchise partners take? I.e. manager, hands-on; professional?
- ✓ Will staff need to be employed?
- ✓ Will staff require any particular skills or attributes?
- ✓ Are franchise partners looking for a substantial business opportunity, or an escape from paid employment?

For this exercise, we will look at two different markets:

- Pet Food Supplier
- Commercial and Domestic Cleaning Company

Let us first consider the pet food supplier. The initial cost of the franchise is unlikely to be high as the income level will be moderate. Having said that, a franchise partner could buy one area, and then expand to several areas by recruiting other delivery drivers and then becoming the overall manager. However, for the purposes of this profile we will assume that the franchise partner only wants to buy one area. The business could be run either full or part time and will be primarily van-based. Staff will probably not need to be employed, and the franchise partners will definitely need to drive! They will also need to be relatively fit as they will most likely be carrying heavy items of pet food to their customers. Good customer services skills and organisational skills will also be important.

The second market is different. This is a management franchise opportunity and therefore the franchise partner profile will be different. The cost of the franchise will be higher as the income potential will also be higher. It is likely to be a full time business; primarily office based and the franchise partner will most likely be the manager. A large number of field staff will need to be employed to carry out the cleaning. The franchise partner will need to be organised, able to manage staff effectively, be good at sales with good communication skills. They will also need to enjoy working as part of a team.

You will see from the above, that your franchise partner profiles are quite different according to which market you are operating in. This will also mean that your marketing plan will need to reflect these messages in order to attract the correct calibre of applicant.

STEP TWO

Recruitment Marketing Plan

When you have completed your ideal franchise partner profile you will be able to include key messages in your marketing materials in order to attract your ideal franchise partners. You will also need to have an understanding of what drives people to buy a franchise so you can reflect these messages. Key drivers include:

✓ Lower risk than starting on your own
✓ Training and on-going support
✓ Known brand
✓ Network support

You now have your ideal franchise partner profile and also an understanding of the drivers to purchasing a franchise. You will also need to consider what you are offering:

- What are you selling to your customers?
- What are you selling to your franchise partners?
- What is your USP?
- Why should they choose you?

Once you are able to answer these questions and you are happy with your value proposition, you are ready to prepare your marketing plan. There are several ways in which you can market your opportunity. I have included the key areas below:

1) **INTERNET**

   The internet is likely to be the most widely used vehicle that prospective franchise partners will look to first, to acquire information. A vast amount of information is available instantly and as a result of this, franchise partners are a lot better informed than previously. They may join forums and check social media sites and blogs. Be mindful of any information that you post on the internet as it is there for a very long time!

It is very important that your franchise opportunity stands out from the plethora of others.

There are several ways in which you can market your franchise opportunity on the internet:

- Your own website
- Specialist franchise websites
- Franchise recruitment websites
- IFA
- BFA
- Non franchise business sites e.g. Businesses for Sale
- Social Media

You can download our free 70 Page guide to Internet Marketing at http://franchiserevolution.co.uk/resources

Let us look at each of these briefly.

a) Your Own Website

This is the obvious place to start, and assuming you already have a website, is free. Prospective franchise partners will be able to learn of your franchise offering as well as browsing your customer site. Some franchisors are reluctant to advertise for franchise partners on their main website for fear of alienating customers. I do not see this as a problem.

If customers are happy with your products and services they will fully understand why you wish to expand.

The main goal at first is to get the email address, phone number and/or full postal address of prospective franchise partners. Sometimes you will only need to offer a prospectus document to obtain their email. You can also try offering an incentive like a sample of your product to get this information. Once you have an email address you can start to market to them. If you decide that Transformative Franchising™ is your franchise development model of choice, then you will also be able to promote the benefits of Transformative Franchising™ to your prospective franchise partners. As mentioned earlier, Franchise Revolution™ has a free e-Booklet specifically aimed at prospective franchise partners that Franchise Revolution™ members can use to promote their franchise.

b) Specialist franchise websites

When searching the internet, most people will only look at the first and second pages of the returned searches. I would therefore strongly suggest that you put yourself in the place of a prospective franchise partner, and type in the search bar what you think they would type when searching for a business opportunity. Then wait and see which specialist franchise sites appear on page one of the searches. Although these websites may cost you more to list your franchise, it will be of benefit to you in the longer term. You also need to consider how much data the website captures about prospective franchise partners. It may be just a name and their contact details in which case a lot of these referrals may not be viable. If you are being charged per referral, you could end up spending a lot of money for little return so check them out first.

c) Franchise Recruitment Websites

These are businesses that specialise in matching franchise partners with franchisors. Once, again carry out the exercise in b) above to see who appears on the first page of the search. Usually, franchise recruitment companies will qualify a prospective franchise partner before referring them onto to you, depending on the information they have received from you. Some will work closely with you, getting to really understand your business and what you are offering. They may be involved from beginning to completion. Others, will just qualify the applicant, and then refer them onto you. Obviously, the former will be more expensive and it is usual for their fee to be a percentage of the initial franchise fee. If you do use a franchise broker, ensure that they follow your franchise recruitment plan and do not make promises over and above those made in the franchise brochure. You may well be liable for any misrepresentation they have made to the franchise partner!

d) IFA & BFA

As mentioned earlier in this E-Book, the IFA and the BFA, offers all franchisors the opportunity of membership, providing certain criteria are met and ensuring that members adhere to a Code of Ethics. The **IFA (http://www.franchise.org)** or the **BFA website (http://www.thebfa.org)** may be the first place a prospective franchise partner will search for opportunities. You will normally need to be a member of these associations in order to be listed on their website.

e) **Non-franchise business for sale sites**

As well as specialist franchise websites, there are also many general business websites for consideration. Perhaps the biggest, and who have a large area dedicated to franchising, is **http://usa.businessforsale.com** and **http://uk.businessesforsale.com**. It is worth bearing in mind, that some prospective franchise partners may not have considered franchising as an option and you will need to think about how you can reach this important target market.

f) **Social Media**

Today, social media is becoming the most popular channel for searching for information and opinions about products and services. People trust other people's opinions on social media sites and forums more than your own marketing messages. So it is essential that you have a strong presence with a Facebook Fan page, a Twitter account and Linkedin Company page. We also recommend that you set up a You Tube channel as video is the most powerful way to promote your business online. If you have products that have a strong visual element, like a restaurant, you should also consider Pinterest for sharing photos.

Once you have set up your social media network you should add daily messages and updates, and ensure you reply to comments from users as soon as possible. You can also join online Linkedin groups where prospective franchise partners might visit and add expert advice with links back to your site. The more you engage online the better as you will build Trust and Authority in your market.

For a complete overview of the internet and how you can get up to speed in only 30 days **download our free 70 Page guide to Internet Marketing at http://franchiserevolution.co.uk/resources**

2) EXHIBITIONS

Taking a stand at an exhibition will probably be the most expensive marketing that you will do. However, this is a real opportunity for you to meet prospective franchise partners face to face. You will be able to showcase your franchise offering and have the opportunity to explain what Transformative Franchising™ is all about putting you ahead of your competition! And if you are a member of Franchise Revolution™ you will be able to offer prospective franchise partners a copy of our e-Booklet as described previously.

Take time to pre-plan and prepare, and this could be the best investment you will make.

a) Franchise Exhibitions

United Kingdom

Franchise Exhibitions are growing in number every year. There are three main exhibitions endorsed by the BFA in the UK. In order to be able to exhibit, you need to be accredited to exhibition status:

- **The British Franchise Exhibition** - usually held in June in Manchester.

- **Franchise Opportunities Live** – usually held in London in September

- o **The National Franchise Exhibition** – usually held in Birmingham (NEC) in October

As well as the above, there are many regional franchise exhibitions that may also be worth considering. These are likely to be cheaper and it may be a good idea to "pilot" a stand to see whether it is an effective marketing medium for you.

Worldwide

The IFA run an annual convention in February of each year, which is held in the U.S. There are numerous exhibitions throughout the U.S and worldwide. **Go to http://franchiserevolution.co.uk/resources** for a full list in the UK and worldwide.

b) **Business and Trade Exhibitions**

As well as specialist franchise exhibitions, there are many other national and local exhibitions that may be worth a try. These include general business expos as well as trade specific exhibitions. Again, they may be cheaper as stated above.

3) **PRESS**

Before the internet explosion, press advertising was the primary vehicle for advertising franchise opportunities. The main two reasons why it is less popular today are that it is very expensive and has a short life span... However, national press exposure may be worth considering, as prospective franchise partners may not be actively seeking a franchise opportunity before spotting your offering. If you decide to advertise in the national press, ensure that you check the newspaper reflects your target market.

It may also be worth you considering placing a well-designed advertisement in respectable franchise magazines. Whilst these do carry a shorter life span than the internet, people that normally purchase these magazines are seriously seeking a franchise opportunity. You will also normally receive full additional coverage in the online version of the magazine.

4) **PRESS RELEASES**

Press releases are an excellent way to raise the profile of your franchise. A press release is:

"A written or recorded communication directed at members of the news media for the purpose of announcing something ostensibly newsworthy. Typically, they are mailed, faxed, *or e-mailed to assignment* editors *at newspapers, magazines, radio stations, television stations, or television networks".* Wikipedia

Your story can be anything newsworthy and may include franchise partner of the year award; charity events; success stories etc. Unfortunately, media providers receive far more press releases than they can publish. To maximise the chances of getting your PR published, you will need to understand how to write a professional PR as well as considering the timing. It may be worth engaging a professional PR agency but remember, although they are far more experienced than you, publication of your PR is still not guaranteed and you may have to pay high fees for the privilege.

5) **WORD OF MOUTH**

Never under-estimate the power of word of mouth advertising. The more people you can tell about your franchise opportunity, the more the word will spread. Talk to your customers, your suppliers and your current core business staff. But most of all, talk to your franchise partners and ask that they spread the word. If you have been integrating Transformative Franchising™ then I am confident your franchise partners will be only too happy to shout from the rooftops about the marvellous opportunity you have! You could also consider running a Franchise Partner Referral Scheme by offering a financial reward to any franchise partner that successfully refers someone to you, who is subsequently recruited to the franchise network. Just ensure that you pay them when you said you would otherwise this can turn into a negative situation!

STEP THREE

Evaluating your Marketing Plan

I will not insult you by saying too much about this step! Suffice to say that you need to ensure that you have a comprehensive and clear evaluation tool for measuring the success of each part of your marketing mix. This will ensure that you maximise your marketing messages and consequently, your recruitment success, by only investing in marketing medium that give you a good return on your investment.

STEP FOUR

Franchise Partner Recruitment Process Flow Chart

This may sound obvious, but can be a really useful tool for tracking your franchise partner recruitment journey as well as ensuring that you do not miss anything. The flow chart should include everything from initial enquiry through to signing the franchise agreement and the accompanying paperwork. Items for consideration are:

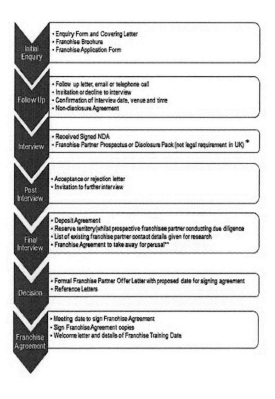

*Franchise Disclosure Pack

At the interview, you will want to allow your prospective franchise partner, to have as much information as possible about your business opportunity to enable them to make an informed decision. A Franchise Disclosure Pack is a more comprehensive Franchise Brochure and so the same conditions apply (see Franchise Brochure earlier in book).

In the UK it is not a legal requirement to have a Franchise Disclosure Pack, but it is very good practice. You should not withhold any pertinent information that may affect the franchise partner's decision to proceed either way. Transformative Franchising™ embeds key principles such as honesty, transparency and trust and these should be reflected throughout the Franchise Disclosure Pack.

Items for consideration in a Franchise Disclosure Pack are:

- Background of business opportunity including the market for the products or services on offer

- Cost of the franchise including working capital

- Detailed franchise partner financial projections to include profit & loss and cash flow

- The terms of the franchise including length of Franchise Agreement; on-going franchise management fees; training and support; renew of franchise; sale of franchise; territory (exclusive or non-exclusive); obligations of the franchisor and franchise partner

- Whether there has been any litigation history

This list is not exhaustive. The Franchise Disclosure Pack should provide all pertinent information to support the prospective franchise partner in making the right decision.

Franchise Agreement. I would suggest that you allow the prospective franchise partner, sufficient time to peruse the Franchise Agreement and to contact a franchise lawyer. I always requested the Franchise Agreement very early on in my research. Many agreements were not of an ethical standard and this saved me lot of time and money much earlier on in the process.

CHAPTER SEVEN

Early Days

The franchise partners have now signed the Franchise Agreement and are part of the franchised network. They are hopefully very excited and looking forward to starting their new business venture with you. The early days of the relationship are vitally important as it is during this time that you need to establish a healthy, professional and collaborative relationship which will hopefully continue throughout the term of the franchise. The two main components here are the initial training and the setup of the franchise partner's business. Let us look at these components in a little more detail.

1) TRAINING

In order for both you and your franchise partners to be successful, you must be able to teach your franchise partners how to confidently replicate the business at all levels.

As mentioned earlier, the initial training experience is one of the first impressions a franchise partner will make about you and your business. It is therefore very important to create the right impression. If you are delivering the training yourself, then ensure that you have the correct skills and attributes. Just because you have built a successful business, does not necessarily mean that you will make a good trainer! The obvious benefits to conducting the training yourself, will be your in-depth knowledge and passion about the business. If someone else has been specifically employed or commissioned for this role, then ensure that they have a thorough understanding of your business, including the "soft" elements such as its philosophy and core values.

It is also very important that you personally conduct some parts of the training in order to develop a relationship with your franchise partners. Identify the specific core skills required to run the business as well as general business skills. In order for you to be successful, it is imperative that your franchise partners are competent in replicating and running all aspects of the business. I would suggest that everyone has a copy of the Operations Manual and that you work through this to ensure that everything is covered. However, please do ensure that you vary the way the training is delivered to ensure you keep the attention of your franchise partners. This can include discussion, role play, video clips, E-Learning and so on. Also have frequent breaks to maintain audience concentration. If possible, you should also try and include different venues including classroom and field visits.

The length of training will depend on the complexity of your business, but broadly speaking I would recommend that you break it into sections:

- **Welcome, Introductions and Background to the Business**
  Firstly, although this may sound obvious, ensure that everyone knows who everybody is and that they feel welcome. The first principle of Transformative Franchising™ is sharing a compelling vision and this is your chance to inspire and motivate your franchise partners and put them into the correct mind-set for the training. I would suggest that you tell your story about how the

business came into being and achieved its current success. You may also like to share your reasons for choosing franchising as a powerful growth strategy. Do not forget to highlight the importance of the role your franchise partners will be playing, in achieving this vision. Include them in the vision. Help them visualise their own business success. Ensure that you talk in a collaborative way – always using "we" and not "I" in your narrative.

- **Business Sector Overview**

  The outcome of this section is to ensure that franchise partners have a thorough overview of the industry sector that they are about to become involved in. They would have most certainly researched this before signing the franchise agreement, and now need a more in depth knowledge. Again, depending on the type of sector you are in, this will vary in complexity. For example, if you are running an estate agency, you would offer an overview of the current property market; key professional bodies such as the National Association of Estate Agents etc. If you were running a care business for older people, then you would offer an overview of the ageing population; how care is currently commissioned; the regulatory bodies such as the Care Quality Commission and so on.

- **Running a Business**

  It is important not to assume that franchise partners are experienced in this area. Even if they have previously run a business it is still important to train them on how to run a business, regardless of their prior experience or knowledge. In this section you would covers items such as finance, sales and marketing, employment law, VAT, insurances, legal compliance and any industry specific legislation. For example, it is no use training a franchise partner in all aspects of delivering your product or service, but neglect to train them on how to market and sell them.

- **Delivering the products or services**

  This is fairly obvious and is the cornerstone of your training. You need to be assured that your franchise partners are both confident and competent in replicating the delivery of your product or service. This section should again include sales and marketing as well as customer service.

- **Franchise Central Office Systems**

  For nearly all types of franchise sectors, there will be specific software and IT systems. For example, the franchisor may have its own internal customer relationship management system but use an external system for payroll and accounts such as SAGE. Franchise partners need to have a good understanding of how each works before leaving the training. However, they would not be expected to remember everything and you therefore need to ensure that they have access to a comprehensive manual to which they can refer to on an on-going basis. The support team will also be able to continue the training in the field.

The above suggestions are not inclusive and you may well want to include different topics in your training. As long as you are confident that your franchise partners are competent in replicating the business and ready to start trading, then you have met your objective. You may want to confirm their competence by setting an end of training test. This is entirely your choice but I would suggest that you do this, as it will identify any weaknesses or shortfalls in particular areas. It will be easier to address these at this point, than later on when there may be problems with the franchise partner's business.

2) SET UP

The formal training has now been completed and the franchise partner is raring to get started! Once again depending on the complexity of the franchise sector, the set up may be minimal. For example, a lawn cutting business will require a liveried van lease; a home office equipped with PC, fax, scanner and telephone; lawn cutting equipment and customers. An estate agency will take longer, as a prominent shop front will need to be found and then refurbished to reflect the franchise brand; staff will need to be employed and so on. However long the set up takes, remember to keep your franchise partners involved and motivated. And remember, they are your partners to success!

CHAPTER EIGHT

Franchise Partner Engagement

Of all of our Transformative Franchising™ strategies, engagement is the most powerful and the most important. The relationship dynamics between the franchisor and franchise partners are very complex. On the one hand, you cannot manage your franchise partners with old fashioned, top-down management techniques. On the other, you cannot expect them to flourish on their own without your support and guidance, as after all they have bought into a franchise and will expect this.

So what do you do? The answer is **Engagement**. Large businesses in the UK, Europe and the US have discovered that the key to sustained high performance from their employees is to engage them in their work. This means that their employees share the same vision and values of their employer, and are committed to their business plan and strategies. They do not just come to work for a pay cheque. They come to work to learn, grow and be fulfilled.

According to extensive research, supported by the UK government **(for more details, go to http://engageforsuccess.org)**, higher engagement levels leads to higher productivity, superior customer service, lower absence and greater wellbeing. Employees work harder and are more innovative. Engaged employees simply perform at a higher level. Disengaged employees cost employers time and money, engaged employees drive business. Engaged employees tend to do more in less time than their disengaged colleagues. The resulting benefits are felt throughout the organisation and beyond: greater productivity, increased customer satisfaction; repeat business; and higher profit for the organisation and its shareholders. Given these facts, it is surprising that most organisations have no engagement plan or strategy, although they believe that engagement impacts business success.

Now take a minute and reread the above paragraph transposing **employees** with **franchise partners**, and you will begin to get the picture.

At Franchise Revolution™, we believe the same is true for franchise partners. To achieve this outcome, a successful Engagement Strategy is required. This is a fundamental change in mind-set for both franchisor and franchise partner.

Franchisor

Currently you may be running a small business with one or two staff. You may have never worked in paid employment, or in a large corporate style business. You may also not have attended any formal training in management, leadership, change management, conflict resolution or any of the plethora of corporate style management and leadership courses. You suddenly find yourself the leader of a growing organisation of franchise partners, as well as a head office, to support the network. Whilst franchise partners are not staff, there are similarities with regard to the leadership qualities they expect from the franchisor as head of the organisation. You may struggle to cope and this may lead to conflict and problems within the network.

Franchise Partners

Some franchise partners may have been employed for most of their lives, and this may be their first step to running and owning their own business. They may look to the franchisor for leadership qualities and may even expect a certain amount of "managing". Even though they are not employees, there are similarities with regard to the leadership qualities they expect from the franchisor, which may lack these key skills.

Other franchise partners are more entrepreneurial and want to be treated as independent business owners. They may resent the franchisor telling them what to do.

For both of the above, the dynamics of the relationship are challenging. Whilst franchise partners are not employees, parts of the franchise agreement will suggest obligations on the part of the franchise partner that may lead them to feel that they are. It is a fine balance to maintain engagement from both franchise partners and the franchisor.

A good starting point is for you to develop Transformational Leadership as the optimal leadership style. Franchisor leadership style greatly impacts on franchise partner brand buy-in. Franchise Revolution™ recommend that franchisors display the following 5 Behaviours to boost engagement with their franchise partners:

1) Demonstrates a clear strategy and direction for the brand, including awareness of competitive threats with a plan to deal with them

2) Are fair and consistent in dealings with all franchise partners, and this means having clear, transparent policies and always upholding them

3) Shows respect by listening to the ideas and concerns of franchise partners before making important decisions. This does not always mean agreeing with them

4) Embodies the values of the brand in everything that they say and do. There must be no hypocrisy. Nothing damages engagement more than hypocrisy.

5) Reminds franchise partners that their profitability is as important as the franchisor's. Everyone in the franchisor's team understands this too.

Professor Merrilees (Professor of Marketing, Griffiths Business School, Australia) endorses the above. He states that franchisor leadership styles can be broadly defined into two styles – transformational or transactional. "Transformational leaders take a radically different approach to getting brand buy-in compared to transactional leaders."

He also explains that "transactional leaders primarily use a simple approach of carrot and stick or rewards and penalties, using tools such as information and marketing support for the brand to get franchisee brand buy-in."

He then goes on to explain that "In contrast, franchisor transformational leaders are more proactive, balancing transactional measures with supportive, emotional methods based on a more caring, interactive and individualised approach, usually with more effective results."

According to Professor Merrilees there are multiple benefits of franchisee brand buy-in. He demonstrates that the research reveals franchisor investment in their brand, and internal branding processes, builds brand equity with both a direct benefit to the franchisor, and an indirect benefit arising from motivating franchisees to invest in the franchisor brand.

Franchise Revolution™ believes that an additional, related benefit of franchise partner engagement is **greater retention of franchise partners**, which is critical to your long-term success.

Professor Merrilees supports this by describing how "lower franchisee exit or churn rates, like lower customer churn rates, reduce the cost of doing business, with less need to recruit and train replacement franchisees."

As he says, "Franchisors can use these research findings to improve franchisee brand engagement with mutually beneficial results for both parties through greater brand equity." This is important research that every franchisor or prospective franchisor should know about, and it was also conducted by Centre Director Professor Lorelle Frazer. **You can read about Professor Merrilees at http://www.franchise.edu.au/bill-merrilees.html** and discover more franchise research findings in the 'Franchise Research' section of the Centre's website at **http://www.franchise.edu.au/franchise-research.html**.

Engage Franchise Partners for Long-term Success

This is when the real work starts, and this is an important part of how Transformative Franchising™ differentiates itself from conventional franchising. According to M.C. Crowley 2011, (Lead from the Heart, Transformational Leadership for the 21st Century), "Engagement is a force that drives human performance. When people are seen as highly engaged, they're influenced to display initiative, approach work passionately and creatively and, essentially, do all they can for their organisation. When engagement is low, people feel less connected and less compelled to put forth extra effort". As discussed in Part One, **transformational leadership is a partnership to reach a higher level of motivation, trust, engagement and empowerment."** (Dr E.J. Shelton 2012, Transformational Leadership - Trust, Motivation and Leadership). Whilst I am not suggesting that employee engagement is exactly the same as franchisee engagement, the similarities are present as we have previously discussed.

Integrating the core principles of transformational leadership into franchising, allows the franchisor to achieve far greater success than following conventional franchising with its primary focus on performance monitoring, compliance, and control. For example, most conventional franchising consultancies will place great focus on the process of developing a franchise, but very little importance on the on-going relationships between the franchisor and franchise partners. This is akin to an employer focusing all of its efforts on recruiting the right employees, and then leaving them to get on with it! So, how can Transformative Franchising™ help you to develop a network of highly motivated and engaged franchise partners? To answer this vitally important question, let us look at each of the Six Principles of Transformative Franchising™ and how these can be integrated into different aspects of the franchisor and franchise partner relationship.

Principle One - Creates a Compelling Shared Vision

"The person, who figures out how to harness the collective genius of the people in his or her organisation, is going to blow the competition away".
Wriston, CEO Citibank (quoted in E.J. Shelton 2012, p.17)

Franchise partners will choose a franchise that they believe in. They will want to feel proud about being part of the brand, and to share the vision. Franchisors need to encourage their franchise partners to continue to share in this vision and to really feel part of it. New innovations, products and services are vital for any business to continue to be successful. Transformative Franchising™ encourages collaboration and contribution from its franchise partners to share their experiences and ideas resulting in a feeling of being valued and listened to.

Principle Two – Puts People First

Whilst I acknowledge that processes and systems do play an integral part in ensuring the success of a franchise, this should **never** take precedence over people. Ultimately, it is your franchise partners that will determine the success, or not, of your business. All too often, support is focused on monitoring the franchise partner for compliance rather than expressing confidence in them. Core values such as trust, respect, and collaboration need to be embedded throughout the central office support team so everybody is aligned to the vision.

Principle Three – Recognises that Engagement is the Key

"Transformational Leadership provides a creative environment, motivation and opportunity to apply skills in a way that benefits their needs as well as the organisations."

(Shelton 2012)

How then, do you ensure that your franchise partners are engaged? Collaboration, contribution and recognition are key drivers in ensuring that franchise partners are motivated and engaged. From talking with franchisees from various sectors, unfortunately these principles are all too often neglected during a support meeting. Instead, issues such as compliance and performance monitoring take precedent, rather than a two way collaborative approach with the franchise partner. Support meetings can of course include an element of monitoring, but this should not be the sole purpose of the visit. You need to be assured that your franchise partners are following your system, protecting your brand, looking after customers and protecting other franchise partners in the network. The key, is how you approach this? When franchise partners understand that you have the greater good of everyone in mind, they are far more likely to remain positive and motivated to work with you and far less likely to try and work against you by potentially bringing your brand into disrepute. Instead, they will want to be part of the success story.

It is vital that the support team are skilled and competent and that franchise partners can see value in the meetings. It is my view that all of your support team should be trained in coaching and mentoring skills to support the personal development of your franchise partners. This may seem like an unnecessary expense at first, but more often than not, the positive outcomes achieved far outweigh the negatives. You will have significantly motivated franchise partners and this will result in greater financial performance for everyone. Interestingly, research into both employee and franchisee motivation, both demonstrates a crossover in that money is not always the key driver to motivation. A feeling of making a difference, feeling valued and listened to, and achieving success (the franchise partners own definition of success, not the franchisor's!), were more important.

The most profitable and rewarding relationships between franchisor and franchise partners are built on trust, integrity and credibility. Always act on these values in everything you do, and you will retain and develop your franchise partners to the highest levels of performance.

Principle Four – Creates Win/Win Outcomes

"Win-win is a frame of mind and heart that constantly seeks mutual benefit in all human interactions. Win-win means that agreements or solutions are mutually beneficial, mutually satisfying."

(Stephen R Covey)

We have already discussed a win/win Franchise Agreement, but how do you achieve win/win franchise partner outcomes?

The answer is to focus on helping your franchise partners get what they want, because if they get what they want then you will get what you want! Every time you have a meeting, or plan a meeting or any interaction with your franchise partners ask this question, "what's in it for them?" and stop asking "What's in it for me?" The more you focus on your franchise partners' needs and outcomes, the more likely you are to achieve a win/win outcome that satisfies both of you.

This seems so easy and obvious, yet it is harder to do in practice. There is a lot of pressure to gain short-term wins and gain advantage. You need to resist these temptations. Always take action based on your vision and values, and take the long-term view. What you may gain today may lead to significant loss in the future, if you act purely out of self-interest.

Principle Five - Leverage Digital Technology

"Through the act of sharing and caring and liking and discussing, we've seen multi-billion dollar businesses created in just a few short years"

D. Priestly (Entrepreneur Revolution, 2013)

It is important that you regularly meet and phone your franchise partners, but you also have other channels available. One of the most powerful tools you have at your disposal for engagement is your website, social media and mobile platforms. You need to be leveraging these powerful tools to their full extent.

We recommend that you blog regularly and ensure that your website features success stories and other news about your franchise partners. You can also set up a private Facebook group or other type of forum for all your franchise partners, where you can discuss important issues and keep everyone updated with the latest news and developments. You also need to Tweet regularly, and set up a private YouTube channel where you can add videos for information, training and other purposes. For immediate, urgent messages why not text your franchise partners to encourage collaboration and connectedness?

The key here is to maintain regular contact with your franchise partners. Connectivity is very important and is evidenced by the massive increase in social media usage over the last few years. You can set up the platforms for this, to be a two-way interaction. Social media, in particular, is the perfect place for consistent engagement and will help to build even stronger relationships.

Principle Six - Encourage Lifelong Learning

"Be not afraid of moving slowly, only of standing still"
(Old Chinese Proverb)

Finally, you can employ the practice and strategy of lifelong learning to foster higher levels of engagement. Extensive research in organisational behaviour has clearly demonstrated that employees are motivated by learning and growing. The same is true for franchise partners, and if you can help them achieve personal growth as well as business growth, both of you will be even more successful.

Learning includes business and product training, but it can be so much more than this. Franchise partners want to earn money and build their businesses, but they may also benefit from learning new personal development skills, which will take them to another level in their lives. They can become even more absorbed in their work and feel like they are progressing beyond their expectations. This is why it is essential to provide the opportunities for your franchise partners to be creative, and to contribute to the development of the overall franchise.

Set up training for "soft skills" like personal development, emotional intelligence and communications skills as well as "hard skills" such as product training. Post inspiring stories and articles on Facebook, and tweet motivational messages and quotes. Always look for ways of inspiring and uplifting your franchise partners, and help them to grow and feel great about themselves.

This section is so important because learning, job satisfaction, overcoming personal challenges and being fulfilled are stronger motivators than money. Maslow's Hierarchy of Needs illustrated this point nearly 60 years ago.

Over the last 10 years there has **been a lot of research** (**read more at http://blogs.hbr.org/cs/2013/04/does_money_really_affect_motiv.html**) which further demonstrates how "extrinsic motivators" like money or awards are less powerful than "intrinsic motivators" like enjoying work or finding meaning. The implications of this research are extraordinary, and explain why Lifelong Learning and Engagement are at the heart of Transformative Franchising™.

Summary

Engaging your franchise partners is your most powerful strategy for long-term, sustained growth. This is why **Engagement** is the central practice in Transformative Franchising™. It leads to improved performance and results that are built on strong values like trust, integrity, fairness and mutual respect. Surely this is the best and only way to build your business?

CONCLUSION

In this final chapter, I want to impress on you why franchising is such a powerful growth strategy for businesses, and why Transformative Franchising™ is the future of franchising. We will review how you can develop a highly profitable, and just as importantly, a highly successful organisation with happy, engaged franchise partners at its' heart.

The Old and New Franchise Paradigms

Franchising, in its current format, is still built predominately on practices such as compliance, control, management and systems. We know that this conventional model can be fraught with problems. We have also learned that there is incontrovertible proof that this approach cannot be sustainable in the future. Intensive research into the benefits of Transformational Leadership over Transactional Leadership (which is more aligned to conventional franchising) has consistently demonstrated, time and time again, that adopting this style of leadership results in a significant increase in employee engagement. This, in turn, leads to a far happier and contented workforce with increased output and therefore ultimately, profit.

We also explored the high correlation between the characteristics of employee engagement and franchisee engagement. Franchise Revolution's new paradigm for franchising is Transformative Franchising™, which embeds the key principles of Transformational Leadership into its heart.

Transformative Franchising™ is the Future

Transformative Franchising™ is different because it focuses on people first, not systems and processes. Transparency, trust, respect and collaboration are key values which flow through every stage of the franchise development journey. The principal message is to treat your franchise partners as "partners". Without them, you simply do not have a franchise.

This does not mean that they have autonomy to do whatever they want to at the expense of the network or brand. It means sharing, collaborating and encouraging your franchise partners to contribute to the growth of the brand as a whole. Maslow's Hierarchy of Needs which was introduced as far back as 1952, clearly demonstrated that once a person acquired the basic needs such as water, food, clothing and warmth, followed then by security (including financial), core principles such as feeling needed, accepted and valued took precedence over the need for money. See diagram below:

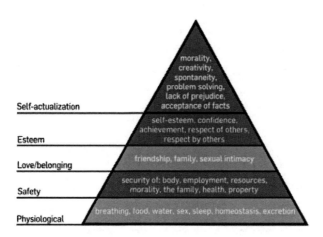

This has been further demonstrated in exit interviews when staff leave an employer. Money was often way down the list as being a reason to leave. Values such as feeling needed, respected and making a meaningful contribution in their work were at the forefront. The Transformative Franchising™ model seeks to embed these principles throughout its practices and teaching.

Franchising is a Powerful Growth Strategy

There are many growth strategies that a business can select for expansion and, in some cases these may be more suited to you than franchising. However, if you like the idea of collaboration and partnerships; not having to invest huge amounts of money; seeing your franchise partners grow and prosper; and growing a substantial, profitable national or international brand that you have created yourself; then franchising is definitely an excellent growth strategy. And Transformative Franchising™ is the right strategy and system to help you achieve your vision.

Not only will you be leveraging your business and taking it to a whole new level of success and profitability, but you will also be developing as an exemplary leader. Transformative Franchising™ encompasses so much more than just growing a brand through processes and systems. By putting people at its heart, you will find your business growing effortlessly (well nearly effortlessly!) and you will be enjoying the journey in the process.

A Review of the 6 Principles

The 6 key principles of Transformative Franchising™ are present throughout this book and pivotal to every idea, strategy and practice you will find here. By following the Transformative Franchising™ framework you will be easily and effortlessly incorporating each principle, as you develop your franchise.

I would now like to take you on a Transformative Franchising™ journey. As you read the following paragraphs, absorb the words and visualise what your business could look like.

"You have developed a very good product or service, and your business is successful and profitable. Your customers rave about your products/services, and your staff love working for you. You know that it is now time to take your business to another, even more successful level. Whilst you enjoy managing your team, you do not want the overall responsibility of managing hundreds of staff by opening several more outlets throughout the country, in order to increase brand awareness. Having spent time investigating the various different growth strategies open to you, you intuitively know that franchising is the right choice and Transformative Franchising™ is the framework that you want to follow. You can visualise a large network of happy, successful and engaged franchise partners. Perhaps you see yourself talking at your annual conference, seeing the sea of happy, motivated franchise partners in the audience. Your brand is now highly visible and respected nationally, and may be internationally too.

You and your franchise partners are working together as a team, as you develop your brand. Collaboration, contribution, trust, respect connectedness, are values that are embedded throughout your organisation. Whilst you care about your own profitability, you are also passionate about the success and profitability of your franchise partners. Celebrations are frequent, as franchise partners reach new levels of success in their own businesses. Everyone is working towards the same goal. Franchise partners are aware of the importance of conducting their businesses in the same way as your core business. There are rarely issues with this, as franchise partners are fully engaged with you, and equally want the brand to develop for the greater good of everyone. You integrate language such as "partnerships", "we" and "our" throughout the organisation to encourage engagement. Your support team are fully conversant with Transformative Franchising™ principles and conduct support meetings collaboratively. Coaching and mentoring skills are prioritised as opposed to management, compliance and control.

You are fully aware of your responsibilities as a transformative franchisor, and your legal documents reflect this. You acknowledge that the Franchise Agreement needs to be weighted in your favour so that you can protect your brand for the greater good of the network and all of its customers. However, the agreement is not onerous, and is written and designed to be fair and equitable, creating win/win outcomes for everyone.

Prospective franchise partners want to join your franchise network as they recognise the opportunity that Transformative Franchising™ can offer them. Your existing franchise partners are ambassadors for your brand.

You recognise that we live in a digital age. You understand the importance of using social media for both your customers and your franchise partners, to encourage communication and connectedness. Your website is professional and reflects the image of your brand. You keep this updated so that customers can be quickly and reliably informed of any new products/services that you may have introduced. You have also set up a forum for franchise partners to communicate with one another, and to share ideas and good practice as well as a Facebook page. You run regular webinars for your franchise partners, which encourage more frequent communication in between face to face meetings and conferences. You are considering developing a mobile phone app. Everyone shares their mobile numbers and email addresses which further encourage open and transparent communication.

Finally, but of great importance, you acknowledge the enormous benefits of lifelong learning for yourself, your staff and your franchise partners. You integrate mentoring and coaching, as well as other forms of personal development, into the support that you offer your franchise partners. You invite motivational speakers to your annual conferences as well as inviting franchise partners to share their own success stories.

The result of all of this? A hugely, successful, happy, sustainable and profitable organisation that everyone is proud to be part of, now and into the future."

This book has been a journey of passion. I stated in the opening pages that I believe franchising to be an excellent model for growth, and that belief is still as strong as ever. I also stated that the conventional emphasis on placing processes and systems before people is outdated, and no longer has a place in our social, digital age.

I also know that there are many existing franchisors that are exemplary models of Transformative Franchising™ even if they do not know it yet! My mission is to encourage all new and existing franchisors to embrace the principles of

Transformative Franchising™. If franchising is to continue to be considered as the powerful growth strategy that it is, then Transformative Franchising™ is the only way forwards.

I wish you the best of luck in your venture.

"Whatever you do, or dream you can do, begin it. Boldness has genius and power and magic in it"

Johann Wolfgang von Goethe

If you think that Transformative Franchising™ may be right for you, then please contact us at **info@franchiserevolution.co.uk** for more information on how we can help your business, or visit our website at **www.franchiserevolution.co.uk**.